FROM SHADOWS

INTO LIGHT

Uncovering the Potential of Citizen Development

COPYRIGHT

Dedication

To my children, Benjamin and Isabella, your presence in my life has changed everything. You've taught me to see the world with wonder, to prioritize what truly matters, and to strive every day to be a better person, because you're watching.

And to my beautiful wife, Mariana, thank you for your unwavering support, love, and patience. Your strength has been my anchor, and your belief in me made this journey possible.

Epigraph

"Innovation doesn't always begin in a boardroom. Sometimes, it starts in silence, in frustration, or a quiet hospital room when you realize there must be a better way."

CONTENTS

AUTHOR BIO

Diego Tuleski is a technology leader and transformation strategist with a passion for empowering nontechnical users to build powerful solutions. With over two decades of experience across business operations and IT, Diego has helped bridge the gap between departments by championing citizen development and AI-enhanced problem solving.

His journey from building unauthorized tools to leading enterprise frameworks reflects the challenges and possibilities of modern digital transformation. Originally from Brazil and now working across global teams, Diego believes that true innovation happens when business and technology grow together.

CHAPTER 1

Shadows Into Light

Back in the 1990s, there was a looming fear that technology would replace people. News headlines were filled with stories about factory jobs being automated, robots replacing workers, and the coming "digital revolution" that would wipe out entire professions.

But even as a teenager, I didn't see it that way.

I believed that technology wouldn't take jobs away; it would change them. And the people who understood how to work with it, rather than fear it, would have a place in the future. That belief, quiet and maybe naïve at the time, is what led me to study computer science.

But studying tech wasn't easy where I grew up. I come from a developing country, and my path was nothing like the Silicon Valley startup founders you hear about. I didn't have access to cutting-edge labs or inspirational professors. I had something much more basic: grit.

To afford college, I had to work full time during the day and study at night. My evenings were spent in classrooms, tired from the workday, often struggling to keep my eyes open. I still remember the embarrassment of nodding off mid-lecture and the silent judgment I imagined from professors and peers. Though truthfully, many of my classmates weren't fully engaged either. For some of them, the goal was just to get the diploma and move on.

There was one exception.

A classmate of mine, fifteen years older than the rest of us, stood out. He was already working full time as a senior analyst at a forestry company and had a clear technical grasp of the material. He paid attention. He asked thoughtful, practical questions. One day after class, he pulled me aside and asked if I might be interested in an internship at his company.

I lit up. My heart jumped.

"Is it in IT?" I asked.

He smiled and said, "Not quite. It's in Sales."

Sales? I hesitated. It wasn't what I was looking for. But something told me not to dismiss it outright. Maybe it was his confidence in me. Maybe it was the fact that someone in the industry thought I was worth recommending.

I said yes, and that yes changed everything.

Of course, I still had to go through the formal interview process. And the truth is, I was wildly unprepared. I was eighteen years old, inexperienced, and overwhelmed. I walked into that interview with more hope than polish. I remember fumbling through some of the answers, unsure if I had made the right impression.

To this day, I still don't fully understand why Tom, the hiring manager, offered me the position. He barely knew me. Maybe he saw potential I hadn't yet seen in myself. Maybe he was taking a chance. Whatever the reason, he gave me a foot in the door, and I never forgot it.

That internship wasn't just a job. It was my first real exposure to the inner workings of a company. It put me on the floor with real problems, real users, and real technology needs. It taught me that value doesn't always come from where you expect it. And it planted the first seed of a truth that would guide me for years:

Innovation doesn't always start in the IT department. Sometimes, it starts where no one is looking.

As it turns out, Tom became one of the best leaders I've ever had the pleasure to work with. He was thoughtful, steady, and trusted people long before they had fully proven themselves. He became not just a mentor, but a friend. He even attended my wedding and now, twenty-five years later, we're still in touch. His belief in me at such an early stage helped shape the career and the person I would become.

The Accidental Breakthrough

The year was 2000. The company ran on an AS/400 system by IBM®, a workhorse of an ERP, but hardly user-friendly. It handled the basics: purchasing, finance, and order management. But it wasn't built for fast answers or flexible reporting.

The Sales team was flying blind. They had no access to real-time sales trends, margin breakdowns, or pricing history. They were making big decisions based on intuition and gut feel.

That's when my classmate, now my boss, introduced me to ODBC connections. We started exploring ways to extract data from the AS/400, transform it with FoxPro, and leverage it in Microsoft® Access. I remember the excitement of seeing structured data, finally ours to manipulate. We started building reports. Then the charts. Then, dashboards long before the term became popular.

The Sales team was amazed. They could now pull their own sales histories. They could compare customers, track regions, and even prepare more accurate forecasts. It was like we'd handed them a flashlight in a dark cave.

Before long, I was offered a full-time role not in IT, but as the guy who could "make the system talk."

Building in the Shadows

Word spread fast. Operations heard about what we were doing. Then Finance. Then the plant floor.

One day, the COO called us in. He had heard that operators at the manufacturing site were still writing production logs by hand.

He asked if we could digitize the process, something that, at the time, felt wildly ambitious.

So we built a simple MES interface that let operators log production data digitally from a local terminal. It wasn't flashy, but it got the job done. The user interface was built in Microsoft Access 2.0, and the underlying data stored in old DBF files was refreshed twice a day. But it worked.

Over time, that basic tool evolved into a full production planning solution. It pulled data from our ERP system, cross-referenced customer orders with available inventory, and began suggesting optimized production schedules.

And here's the thing: we were solving real problems.

But we were doing it completely outside of IT.

No version control. No documentation. One shared database. Backups? ZIP files saved on a shared drive with the date in the filename. It was fast, effective, and unsanctioned.

We weren't trying to rebel. We were trying to help.

But to IT, we were dangerous.

Heroes to the Business, Villains to IT

To the business, we were problem solvers. People who got things done when others said, "That's not my department."

To IT, we were something else entirely: rogue developers. A risk to the company's stability. A shadow team was creating technical debt faster than it could be discovered.

At the time, I didn't understand their frustration. I saw their caution as bureaucracy. I didn't see the bigger picture, security, scalability, long-term support.

I thought we were just helping.

But years later, I would come to see both sides and realize that the truth is more complicated.

CHAPTER 2

The Rise and the Fallout

For a while, we were unstoppable.

The Sales team saw us as miracle workers. The operations folks couldn't believe how quickly they could get real-time insights. Even upper management started to rely on our reports during monthly meetings. We weren't just reacting to requests anymore, we were anticipating them: building dashboards, automating updates, creating tools that people didn't even know they needed.

We weren't working in IT, but it sure felt like it.

We had momentum. Trust. A backlog of requests. And a growing sense of purpose.

But looking back now, it's easy to see what we were missing: structure.

No proper versioning. No formal support model. No disaster recovery plan. Just a growing pile of "successes" built on fragile foundations.

And sooner or later, it was all going to catch up with us.

The Fragile Empire

As our solutions spread, so did our exposure.

We were now touching nearly every function: Sales, Operations, Customer Service, and even elements of Finance. And yet, our entire architecture was duct-taped together. Sometimes, literally an old PC in the corner acting as a "server," accessed by mapped drives and hard-coded paths.

There were days when I'd come into work and see the blue screen of death on that machine. My stomach would drop. I'd rush to reboot it, hoping it hadn't taken down a dashboard someone needed for a presentation.

One time, a report failed during a quarterly business review with regional managers. A VP looked at the empty chart and said, "Did IT break it?"

I wanted to explain that this wasn't IT's system, it was mine. But I stayed quiet.

That's when it hit me: we were supporting a growing digital ecosystem without the infrastructure, processes, or safety nets.

And we were running out of time.

The Exit That Sparked the Collapse

Seven years into this journey, I made a bold decision: to move abroad and study English in Dublin, Ireland. It wasn't part of a corporate plan or international assignment; it was a personal choice, driven by a desire to grow, challenge myself, and explore new horizons. I knew it would mean stepping away from the momentum I had built, but I also knew it was the right time to expand my perspective and invest in myself.

I gave three months' notice. During that time, I trained my replacement, documented key reports, and even created a few how-to guides. It wasn't perfect, but I genuinely believed I was leaving things in good shape.

Then I left.

It had only been two weeks since I'd officially left the company. I was already out of the country, trying to settle into a new chapter of my life, when my phone rang. The caller ID showed a familiar number from an IT member of a team that, not long ago, had barely acknowledged the tools I had built.

Now they were calling me. Not casually. Desperately.

They were overwhelmed. The very systems they had once dismissed as rogue, unsupported, or risky had become deeply embedded in daily operations. And without me around to maintain them, things were starting to break.

I could hear the stress in their voices. Critical processes were failing. Reports weren't running. Teams downstream were escalating.

They didn't offer compensation. They didn't have to. I never even brought it up.

I felt responsible because, in many ways, I was. These were tools I had created in the shadows, without support, documentation, or backup plans. They had served their purpose, yes, but I had left behind a fragile infrastructure with no safety net.

So I said yes. I didn't hesitate.

They granted me VPN access, and I logged in remotely from across the world. I walked them through troubleshooting steps, rebuilt broken logic, and restored corrupted databases. It was surreal guiding the very team that had once kept me at arm's length, now relying on me to keep the business running.

And in that moment, I realized just how thin the line was between shadow and critical.

What I had built wasn't just a workaround anymore. It had become part of the system.

That experience didn't just reinforce my belief in business-led innovation, it also solidified my conviction that it must be done responsibly, with transparency, support, and a sustainability plan.

The Cost of Informal Innovation

Not long after that, IT made the decision to bring in a consulting firm to take over the systems I had built. It was a logical step: formalize the support, reduce the dependency on a single individual, and try to bring those shadow tools into the light.

But it came at a cost, literally.

The consultants charged a premium. What had been developed on nights and weekends with no budget now required a six-figure contract just to stabilize. It was a painful but necessary lesson: when solutions are built outside the system, they may solve the problem fast, but eventually, someone pays the price to bring them back into alignment.

That experience helped shape my belief that business-led innovation doesn't just need to be empowered, it needs to be planned, supported, and sustainable from day one.

The consultants spent months dissecting what I had built, reverse engineering flows, rebuilding reports in enterprise-grade tools, and documenting dependencies that had never been written down.

It cost the company more than I'd like to admit, not just in consulting fees, but in lost time, missed insights, and frustrated users.

And still, the solutions they created weren't as flexible or as fast. They were "official," but they weren't tailored to the business like ours had been.

I watched from afar, both proud and conflicted. Proud of what we had done. Conflicted by how fragile it had been.

CHAPTER 3

Reflection in Recovery

Before I could step into the next chapter of my professional life, one shaped by new confidence, fresh perspective, and a stronger command of English, I was forced to pause.

Just two weeks after arriving back from Dublin, while staying with my parents and actively interviewing for what felt like the next big leap in my career, life delivered an unexpected and deeply personal detour.

I was in the final rounds with two major multinationals. These were the kinds of roles I had envisioned when I decided to study abroad, positions that promised growth, challenge, and international exposure. I remember the nervous energy of checking my email constantly, rehearsing responses, picturing myself stepping into a new chapter.

But then everything stopped.

What started as lingering back pain and restless nights quickly became something more serious. I visited several doctors many thought it was muscular. But my resting heart rate hovered around 120, and deep down, I knew something wasn't right. It wasn't until I saw a pulmonologist, who ordered a chest X-ray, that things began to unravel. The X-ray showed something unusual: a foggy shadow that turned out to be a pleural effusion. An MRI confirmed the source of a tumor. The diagnosis came shortly after: lymphoma.

That same day, as I lay in a hospital bed with IVs in my arm and fear beginning to settle in, one of the companies I'd interviewed with called to offer me the job. It was a dream role at a prestigious automotive company I had long admired.

I declined immediately. I told them it was due to health reasons, though I didn't go into detail. It was one of the hardest conversations I've ever had. I wasn't turning it down because I didn't want it, but because I knew I wouldn't be able to give it everything it required. My path had changed.

The following months were nothing like I had planned, but they changed me in ways I could never have anticipated.

Finding Clarity in Crisis

In that stillness, life slowed down. My world shrank to a hospital room, a handful of familiar faces, and a calendar that revolved around treatment cycles.

But even in that compressed world, something strange happened: time moved both slower and faster. While my body rested, my mind raced. I found myself replaying old projects, thinking about the dashboards, the tools, the systems I had built over the years. They had made people's lives easier, but now I saw how fragile they were. They worked, but they weren't sustainable. They were held together with duct tape and hope.

When something like this happens, everything slows down and, strangely, speeds up. Each day blurs into the next, yet your mind races. Even in that stillness, mine stayed active.

I remember one night, after another round of blood tests, I asked the nurse in charge if I could access their internal system. She gave me a quick tutorial on how to navigate the interface, a clunky black screen with green text, like something out of a forgotten era. But to me, it was a window. I started reviewing my red and white blood cell counts, platelets, and whatever data I could find. I documented everything by hand. Then, back in bed, I opened my laptop and built a small database to track the trends.

I knew I was just one data point, that this wouldn't hold up to scientific scrutiny, but I couldn't help myself. I began charting changes, speculating about the influence of nutrition, treatments, and even sleep. I shared the graphs with nurses and dietitians. They were kind, even humored me, but I knew this wasn't about discovering anything groundbreaking.

It was about staying engaged. It was about staying with me.

A Call from the Past

Then, one day, the phone rang.

It was someone from the same company I had worked for before Dublin. They'd heard I was back and they needed help. The systems I had built years ago, quietly and unofficially, were still in use. But now, without someone to maintain them, they were starting to fall apart.

They asked if I could support the team remotely, troubleshooting, updating, and keeping things running.

I never asked whether the call was really about the systems or if it was their way of helping me stay mentally anchored during such a difficult time. Maybe it was both. Maybe it didn't matter.

What mattered was that it gave me something to hold on to.

So there I was sitting in a hospital bed, hooked up to IVs, a laptop on my lap, debugging code, rebuilding queries, answering questions, solving problems. It gave my days structure. It gave me purpose. And in its quiet way, it gave me space to reflect.

Seeing It All More Clearly

For the first time, I had distance from my work, physical, emotional, and mental distance. And with that came clarity.

I saw how much we had accomplished, but also how fragile it all was. The systems had delivered value, yes. But they were built outside the process, unsupported, undocumented. No one could truly maintain them because no one else understood how they worked.

And that wasn't innovation. That was a risk.

I had spent years trying to empower people, solve problems, and move fast. But now, in the stillness of recovery, I realized something deeper:

It wasn't enough to build. We had to build responsibly.

It wasn't just about creating solutions, it was about creating sustainable, secure, shared capability. I began to see shadow IT not as something to be proud of or ashamed of, but as a signal. A signal that the business had needs that IT hadn't been able to meet.

The problem wasn't what we built. The problem was how we built it, and the fact that we built it in isolation.

That realization stayed with me.

From Patient to Practitioner

As I got stronger, I kept working. The hospital staff got used to seeing me with a laptop. Nurses would ask what I was doing; doctors would joke that I was probably rebuilding the hospital's scheduling system.

One of the nurses I saw regularly became a close companion during that time. Her name was Simin, and she was originally from Iran. She had a calm presence and a quiet warmth that made even the hardest days feel a little lighter. She often passed by my room and saw me typing away, intensely focused on lines of code or dashboards. One day, with a smile, she said, "You remind me of my daughter, she's also in IT. I think you two would get along."

That moment led to a surprising connection.

Her daughter, Karina, turned out to be a team leader at a large SAP® consulting firm. Simin arranged the introduction, and soon Karina and I were talking about systems, technology, and transformation from the perspective of two professionals who had taken very different paths to similar places.

We also became friends and remain so to this day.

It's funny how life works. Amid treatment and uncertainty, a chance encounter in a hospital room led to a connection that shaped not only my recovery but my network and reminded me that even in our hardest seasons, we can find new doors quietly opening.

I wasn't just recovering physically, I was rethinking everything.

By the time I finished treatment and was declared in remission, I was a different person. Not just in body, but in mindset.

I still believed in business-led innovation. But now I knew, with absolute certainty, that it had to be done with structure, with partnership, and with a long-term view.

That insight would shape everything that came next, from joining the IT department to building the citizen developer framework that would redefine how our organization worked.

But it started here.

In a hospital room. With a laptop. And a realization that even in the most unexpected places, clarity can find you.

Inside the System I Once Bypassed

Then one day, seemingly out of the blue, I received a call from someone in HR.

We exchanged a bit of small talk about how things were going, how I was adjusting after returning from Ireland, and then came a question I didn't expect, but one that would quietly change the course of my career:

"Would you ever consider joining the IT department?" At first, I laughed half out of surprise, half out of disbelief. Me? In IT? After all the workarounds I'd built, all the shortcuts and unsanctioned solutions I had championed? I had spent years navigating around IT, not inside it.

But as I sat with the question, I realized something had shifted. I had seen the gaps. I had felt the tension from both sides. And more than anything, I had come to understand that the divide between business and IT wasn't just a technical one, it was cultural. And maybe, just maybe, I could help bridge it. So I paused, took a breath, and said something that surprised even me:

"Yes. I think I would."

Of course, not everyone was thrilled about the idea. The IT Manager at the time, let's call him Mario, had every reason to be skeptical. For years, he had viewed my work as a constant disruption. From his perspective, I was the guy who built fragile, undocumented solutions that complicated support, created technical debt, and made IT's job harder. He didn't just disapprove of what I had done, he actively resented it.

So when HR brought up my name as a candidate to join the department, his first reaction wasn't excitement, it was frustration. He pushed back. He challenged my track record. He asked, "Why would we bring in someone who caused half of the mess we're trying to clean up?"

But something shifted in those conversations. Maybe it was the realization that I knew the business better than most, or that I could speak both "languages." Maybe it was his leadership maturity showing. Whatever it was, Mario eventually agreed to bring me in. And over time, our relationship transformed.

The tension gave way to trust. He saw how committed I was to doing things the right way, and I saw how deeply he cared about protecting the integrity of our systems. What started as quiet tolerance turned into real collaboration. Eventually, we built a solid partnership. And even more than that, he became a great friend.

It's still one of the most meaningful full-circle moments in my career: being hired by the very person who once wanted nothing to do with me. Not because I proved him wrong, but because we chose to work together to build something better.

Crossing the Line

It felt like a full-circle moment.

I had started in Sales. Built tools for Operations. Operated in the shadows. Now, I was being invited to step into the system I had worked around for so long.

And I accepted.

My time in IT taught me things I never knew I needed: about governance, about architecture, about the importance of process, not just to slow things down, but to keep things running. I began to understand what IT had been trying to protect all along. But I also realized something equally important:

What I had done, the good and the bad, wasn't unique. It was inevitable.

Because when business teams don't have the tools they need, they'll find ways to create them.

They'll hack, automate, and cobble things together. Not because they're rebellious, but because they're resourceful.

And unless IT finds a way to support that energy to shape it instead of suppressing it, they'll always be chasing shadows. That's when the seed of a new idea was planted.

Not about shutting down shadow IT but about replacing it with something better.

CHAPTER 4

Crossing Over to IT

I t felt like the ultimate plot twist.

For years, I had been the person IT warned others about, not maliciously, but warily. I was the "guy who built stuff outside the system," the one who launched tools without formal approval, who made things work when the official way took too long.

Then one day, I found myself sitting across the table from the IT manager who had once openly opposed everything I represented.

He didn't sugarcoat it.

"I didn't like what you did," he told me. "You broke the rules. You made us nervous. You built systems we couldn't see or control."

I nodded. He wasn't wrong.

But then he said something I didn't expect:

"But I've also seen the impact. And if we can channel that same energy inside the guardrails we could get ahead."

That conversation was the beginning of everything. He took a risk on me, and I took a risk on joining a world I'd once operated outside of. We were skeptical of each other at first, but over time we found common ground. Eventually, that manager became not just a colleague but a mentor and a friend.

When I walked into the IT department on my first official day, I expected to feel a sense of arrival. After all, I had spent years dancing around the edges of IT building tools, solving problems, and earning respect from the business. I thought joining IT would feel like coming home.

It didn't.

It felt like walking into a different language, a different culture, and, honestly, a different mindset.

Where I had learned to move fast and fix things, IT moved carefully and avoided breaking things. Where I had been praised for improvising, IT prioritized predictability. Where I had worked with business users every day, many of my new colleagues hadn't stepped into a plant or sales office in years.

It wasn't better or worse, just different.

And I realized right away: I had a lot to learn.

Learning the Language of IT

My first few months in IT were humbling. I sat through architecture reviews where I barely understood the acronyms. I listened to discussions about capacity planning, disaster recovery, cybersecurity audits, and multi-tiered system redundancy.

I realized how little I had understood about the risks we'd been creating in the name of agility.

For the first time, I saw the business from the other side. I saw how fragile even a small break in a core system could be. I saw how many layers were needed to keep the company secure, compliant, and operational across global locations.

And I began to understand why IT had always looked at us, at me, with so much caution.

We hadn't just been rogue developers.

We had been building a second, unofficial infrastructure inside the company.

No wonder they were worried.

The Missing Link

While I was absorbing everything IT had to offer, governance, process discipline, and long-term planning, I also began to see something missing:

Innovation.

Not innovation in the tools or technologies, IT had plenty of that, but innovation in how problems were solved day to day.

The business was still submitting tickets for basic needs: a report tweak, a form change, a minor automation. And those tickets sat in queues, often for weeks.

I knew from my own experience that many of those business users could solve their problems if only they had the tools and guardrails.

The business was getting more tech-savvy. Tools were getting more user-friendly. Cloud platforms were changing the game. But there was no structure to support this shift.

And here I was, sitting in IT, finally in a position to change that.

A Pivotal Move

As the company continued to grow and evolve, so did my career. One of the most significant milestones came when I was offered the opportunity to relocate to the United States.

At the time, the organization was preparing for a major transformation: rolling out a new ERP system across our North American operations. Brazil had just completed its SAP implementation, and I had been deeply involved in that journey. I wasn't the most experienced SAP expert, but I had something that set me apart: I understood the system, I understood the business, and I could communicate clearly in English.

Right man, right place, right time.

The decision to move wasn't easy. It meant leaving family, comfort, and familiarity behind. But it also meant growth, a chance to lead, to influence a new region, and to bring everything I had learned to a larger stage.

I was asked to lead the team responsible for supporting the SAP implementation in North America. It wasn't just a technical role, it was a bridge between cultures, between teams, and between business needs and system capabilities. I found myself once again translating not just between languages but between priorities, expectations, and ways of working.

That experience would shape me profoundly. It gave me new confidence. It helped me see problems from a broader, more strategic perspective. And it reaffirmed something I had long suspected: being able to connect the dots across geographies, systems, and people was a rare and valuable skill.

It was in this new context, working across borders, building new teams, and navigating growing complexity, that the seeds for my next big insight began to take root.

The "Aha" Moment

One day, during a routine meeting with a supply chain analyst, I had a moment that changed everything.

She was frustrated. She needed to automate a repetitive task, something she did every Monday morning, but the IT ticket she submitted had been sitting untouched for three months.

"I could build this in Excel if I just had access to the data," she said.

And that's when it hit me.

She wasn't asking for permission to break things. She was asking for permission to help.

That's when I had the thought:

What if we didn't fight this? What if we designed for it?

Instead of shutting down business-led solutions, what if we supported them?

What if we could create a model where business users were enabled to build within a structured, governed environment?

What if IT stopped being the bottleneck and became the enabler?

That was the spark that would eventually become our Citizen Developer program.

But it started with one question:

What if shadow IT wasn't the enemy? What if it was untapped potential?

Bridging Two Worlds

I began talking to people quietly at first. A few leaders in IT. A few colleagues from my old business network. I asked about their pain points, their fears, and their ideas.

What I found was striking:

Business users wanted more control but not chaos.

Many business users had grown tired of bottlenecks. They were the ones closest to the problems, tracking orders, resolving customer issues, balancing inventories, yet they felt powerless to improve the systems that shaped their daily work. What they asked for wasn't unrestrained access or the ability to circumvent IT. What they wanted was the freedom to act on their insights, to build what they needed without drowning in red tape. But they also recognized the need for structure. They didn't want to be responsible for breaking critical systems or creating redundant tools. What they needed was permission with purpose control within a framework, not chaos disguised as empowerment.

IT Teams Wanted Oversight but Not Overload

On the other side, IT teams were stretched thin. Their backlog was growing, infrastructure needed maintenance, and the pace of change in the business kept accelerating. The idea of business-led development initially triggered alarm: more platforms to manage, more security risks to monitor, more unknowns introduced into an already complex environment. But most IT professionals weren't opposed to innovation. Many were relieved at the idea of teams solving their problems if it could be done safely. What they wanted was visibility. They needed to know what was being built, where the data lived, and how it would affect enterprise systems. With the right governance in place, IT didn't feel threatened by citizen developers; they felt supported by them.

Everyone wanted faster solutions, but no one wanted to compromise security or stability.

Across the organization, there was agreement on one thing: speed mattered. In a fast-moving business environment, delays in automating processes, adjusting reports, or launching tools translate directly into lost opportunities and frustrated teams. People were done waiting months for basic improvements. But they also knew what was at stake. A poorly designed app that exposed sensitive data or caused a system conflict wasn't just inconvenient, it was dangerous. What everyone wanted was speed with safety solutions that could be delivered faster because they were built closer to the problem, but still designed with stability and compliance in mind.

The problem wasn't that our goals were misaligned.

The problem was that we hadn't created a shared model for building together.

What I Knew for Sure

After spending years working inside IT and years working outside it, I had a unique vantage point. I'd seen both worlds. I'd been a business user trying to make things work with the tools I had, and now I was an IT insider trying to keep systems stable while demands poured in from every direction.

And from that vantage point, I came to understand three things with absolute clarity:

1. IT wasn't the enemy. They were doing the best they could with limited resources and a heavy responsibility.

When I was on the business side, it was easy to get frustrated with IT. Delays felt like resistance. Policies felt like roadblocks. But once I stepped into their world, I saw the pressure they were under. IT wasn't dragging its feet, they were protecting the core. They were responsible for security, compliance, uptime, support, architecture, vendor contracts, and more. Their job wasn't just to build things; it was to keep everything running even when no one noticed. What looked like bureaucracy from the outside was often the only thing standing between business continuity and serious risk. Their caution wasn't a lack of interest; it was a form of stewardship.

2. Business users weren't reckless. They were solving problems the only way they knew how.

On the IT side, I often heard concerns that business users would break things, misuse data, or create more work for support teams. But having been one of those users myself, I knew that wasn't the full picture. Business users didn't wake up thinking, How can I go around IT today? They were just trying to do their jobs better. They used spreadsheets, forms, macros, whatever they could find because they couldn't wait for help that might take weeks or never come at all. They were resourceful, not rebellious. And given the right tools and support, they were capable of contributing meaningful solutions, ones that IT might never think to build on its own.

3. There had to be a better way.

A way that didn't put IT and the opposition business. A way that didn't force a false choice between control and creativity, between speed and stability. What we needed wasn't less oversight or more freedom; it was a shared approach, one that gave the business the ability to act and IT the confidence that what was being built could scale safely. A model where everyone had a role, a voice, and a shared stake in digital innovation. We needed something new, not just in tooling or training, but in mindset. A culture of co-creation.

And I realized: with my background, my time in the shadows, and now inside the system, I was in a unique position to help create that bridge.

A bridge built on trust, enablement, and governance.

And so the next chapter of my journey began not as a rebel or an outsider, but as a reformer, working from within.

Not long after, I started drafting what would become our first Citizen Developer framework.

CHAPTER 5

The Aha Moment

Ideas don't always arrive like lightning bolts. Sometimes they creep in, quietly built from years of experience, frustrations, and little flashes of clarity that slowly begin to connect.

This one started in a conversation over coffee.

A business user from the Finance team had built a personal macro in Excel to generate a weekly report. It wasn't fancy, but it saved her hours every week. I asked if she had shared it.

She hesitated. "I thought about it," she said, "but I didn't want to get in trouble."

That sentence stuck with me.

Not "I didn't want to break anything."

Not "I didn't think it would help."

"I didn't want to get in trouble."

In that moment, I realized how deeply ingrained the fear of shadow IT was. We had spent years telling business users not to build, and now we were surprised when they didn't innovate.

I wasn't alone in this realization. Around this time, I had a colleague, a great partner in crime named Felipe. He had been seeing the same patterns, feeling the same frustrations, and quietly thinking about what could be done differently. When I brought up the idea of structured, supported business-led development, he didn't need convincing; he got it immediately.

Felipe fully understood the challenge: business users wanted to help but were being held back by fear, ambiguity, and a lack of support. He agreed something had to change. And, more importantly, he was willing to help me figure out how.

Having a partner who shared the vision was more than helpful; it was fuel. Felipe challenged assumptions, validated ideas, and helped shape the early version of what would become our Citizen Developer framework. In many ways, the spark of this movement didn't come from just one "aha" moment; it came from shared insight and shared purpose.

The Energy Was Already There

The truth is, citizen development was already happening.

You could see it in:

- The macros people built to clean up data
- The shared spreadsheets used as makeshift CRMs
- The Power BI dashboards are quietly published to Teams
- The hundreds of Zapier™, n8n and Power Automate flows that popped up like mushrooms after the rain

Business users were solving real problems, just under the radar. Quietly. Alone.

The energy was there.

What was missing was a structure to harness it, guide it, and protect it.

That was my "aha" moment.

We didn't need to suppress this movement.

We needed to build a runway for it.

A New Vision for IT

I started sketching. Literally. On napkins, whiteboards, notebooks any surface I could find.

What if IT didn't try to stop business-led innovation... ...but made it safer, faster, and more impactful?

What if we created a framework that empowered users to build, with the right tools, boundaries, and support?

And what if IT became a platform team, not just a service desk, offering governance, coaching, and infrastructure that enabled the business to innovate safely?

I wasn't thinking of it as a formal program yet. But the idea had taken hold.

We needed a third space between full code IT development and no rules shadow IT.

We needed a framework for business-led development with enterprise-level guardrails.

Discovering the Term: Citizen Developer

At the time, I hadn't heard the term "citizen developer." But as I researched what others were doing in this space, I came across it first in a white paper, then in a Microsoft talk, and eventually in conversations with peer companies.

The concept clicked immediately.

A citizen developer wasn't trying to build the next SAP. They weren't bypassing IT maliciously. They were solving targeted problems with the tools available to them, responsibly, when given the chance.

And with the right support, they could build high-impact tools, automate painful processes, and unlock new capacity across the business.

The light bulb went off.

"We don't need to eliminate citizen developers.

We need to develop them.

The Tension That Sparked Transformation

Around this time, I started informally floating the idea with colleagues, both in IT and the business.

Some got it right away. They had stories of business users who had built clever tools, only to be shut down. They saw the value in a more formal approach.

Others were skeptical.

- "How will we manage risk?"

- "What if people build the wrong thing?"
- "Isn't this just going to create more work for us later?"

These were valid concerns. And they shaped how I thought about the program.

If we wanted citizen development to scale, it had to be:

Secure by design

Security couldn't be an afterthought. If we were going to allow business users to build their solutions, some of which might access sensitive data or integrate with critical systems, then the foundation had to be secure from day one. This meant setting up the right permission models, ensuring data access was governed, and applying policies at the platform level, not just relying on education or trust. Security couldn't depend on individual judgment. It had to be baked into the environment itself, so that every app built, no matter how simple, operated within safe boundaries. When people know they can build confidently without risking compliance or data exposure, they're more likely to engage, and IT is more likely to support them.

Aligned with IT principles

This wasn't a parallel universe. For the program to survive and thrive, it needed to respect the core principles of enterprise IT: system integrity, sustainability, performance, and maintainability.

That didn't mean business users had to become architects. But it did mean their work had to align with the broader architecture. We needed naming conventions, lifecycle management, reusability standards, and clear integration protocols. Citizen development couldn't be a loophole; it had to be a branch of the broader technology strategy. That's what would make it scalable and respected, not just tolerated.

Supported by Training, Mentorship, and Prioritization

One of the early lessons we learned was that simply granting access to a low-code platform didn't automatically translate into results. The tools might be intuitive, but building meaningful solutions still requires thought, structure, and support.

Citizen developers didn't just need documentation, they needed real guidance. They needed examples that mirrored their business context, templates to accelerate their learning, feedback loops to course correct quickly, and most importantly, access to people who could help them grow. That's why we introduced the concept of IT champions, technical mentors embedded in the process. Their role wasn't to build for the business, but to build up the business. They acted as coaches, advisors, and enablers, helping citizen developers turn ideas into robust solutions.

But there was another reality we couldn't ignore: not everything could be built at once.

As the program gained traction, more and more use cases emerged. Some were simple, others required integration with enterprise systems, or access to sensitive data. And in those cases, IT was still required to step in, whether for architecture reviews, security assessments, or API enablement. That meant we needed a way to manage the pipeline of ideas.

We developed a prioritization process, a lightweight but structured approach to evaluate new proposals. Using a simple matrix that measured effort versus return, we helped citizen developers understand which ideas to tackle first and which ones might need to wait. This wasn't about shutting down innovation, it was about channeling it where it could have the greatest impact.

By combining mentorship with prioritization, we found a sweet spot: business users felt empowered and guided, and IT maintained the visibility and capacity to support what mattered most. It kept the momentum going, avoided burnout, and created a more strategic path for scaling the program sustainably.

Embedded into the Governance Fabric of the Organization

Citizen development couldn't live off to the side as a "cool experiment." It had to be woven into how the company worked from intake to support, from security reviews to executive dashboards. That meant formalizing the process: including citizen apps in governance meetings, tracking them in IT inventories, monitoring their usage, and defining thresholds for escalation. By embedding citizen development into the governance structure, we weren't just legitimizing it, we were making it part of the company's digital DNA. This integration is what made IT feel safe and made the business feel supported.

We didn't need a revolution. We needed a rethink.

The First Sketches of a Framework

That's when the framework started to take shape.

It wasn't about tools. It was about trust. It wasn't about decentralization. It was about distributed innovation, governed centrally.

We knew that empowering the business to build couldn't come at the expense of security, stability, or alignment. So we began outlining the foundational elements of a model that would enable responsible innovation at scale.

Here's what we designed:
- A tiered model to categorize apps by risk and complexity
- Clear roles: citizen developer, IT champion, governance lead
- Approved platforms, starting with Microsoft Power Platform
- a useful training path, not just compliance-focused
- A plan to monitor, measure, and support apps after they launch

And, perhaps most critically, a lightweight intake and approval process.

To make this process fast, fair, and effective, we created a small review committee, a cross-functional group designed to quickly assess use cases as they were proposed. Their mission wasn't to gatekeep. It was to provide a green light or course correct early, so no one wasted time or introduced unnecessary risk.

This committee looked at three things:

1. Risk exposure – Would the solution put sensitive data or core systems at risk?

2. System alignment – Would it conflict with or duplicate existing enterprise tools?

3. Process owner support – Did the business function responsible for the process support the solution?

With that structure in place, ideas could be vetted quickly and transparently. And more importantly, developers got timely feedback and a clear path forward.

This wasn't shadow IT. This wasn't "DIY everything. This was something new:

A structured, supported, scalable way to let the business build, without breaking what holds us together.

The Shift in Identity

For the first time in my career, I saw myself not as someone caught between IT and the business, but as someone who could connect them.

And I realized: if we did this right, we could change the relationship between business and IT forever.

No longer gatekeepers. No longer rebels.

Partners. Co-creators. Innovators.

CHAPTER 6

Designing the Citizen Developer Framework

The idea was clear. The momentum was building. But now came the hard part: turning a vision into a working model.

It's one thing to talk about empowering business users.

It's another thing entirely to create a framework that enables them to build solutions safely, responsibly, and at scale, without overwhelming IT or introducing unnecessary risk.

Fortunately, we weren't starting from scratch or starting alone.

Our global CIO at the time, Leandro San Miguel, was both open-minded and curious—a rare and powerful combination in leadership. Originally from Salta, Argentina, he had moved abroad more than two decades earlier, but his identity as a *salteño* remained ever-present. People from Salta are known for their warm hospitality, strong sense of heritage, and deep pride in their land—and Leandro embodied all of that with quiet confidence.

From our earliest conversations, he showed a sincere willingness to explore what citizen development could mean for the organization. But he also brought something equally important: a grounded, pragmatic perspective. His ability to balance visionary thinking with practical execution made him a steady and influential force as we navigated uncharted territory.

Leandro didn't say "no." Instead, he asked the right questions, the kind that surfaced the technical, operational, and security concerns we would need to address from the start. Together, we identified the architectural and cybersecurity pillars that would shape the direction of the program:

Architecture: usability, scalability, reusability, maintainability, support, impact analysis, and stability

Cybersecurity: confidentiality, integrity, and availability

Another key ally in this journey was Matt, our VP in charge of HR and EH&S at the time. Matt immediately saw the potential of the program not just from a strategic or digital transformation perspective, but from lived experience.

His background as a former plant manager gave him a frontline view of the inefficiencies and manual workarounds happening daily on the shop floor. He was energized by the idea of turning problem solvers into solution builders. He didn't just support the concept, he couldn't wait to get started. Within days, he was already identifying one of his team members to be trained as a citizen developer.

More than that, Matt recognized that for the program to succeed, it needed structure and ownership. He actively championed the creation of a new role within IT, someone dedicated to coordinating the program, mentoring developers, supporting platforms, and driving adoption across the business. That investment changed everything. It signaled that this wasn't a hobby project; it was a strategic initiative, with visible executive backing.

With both executive curiosity and operational support, we had the foundations we needed.

Now, it was time to build.

Architecture and Security Foundations

On the architecture side, we had to think about:

Usability – Would these tools be intuitive enough for business users?

Scalability – Could small solutions grow without being rebuilt from scratch?

Reusability – Could components be shared across teams or regions?

Maintainability & Support – Who would own the app once it was launched?

Impact Analysis & Stability – How could we ensure changes wouldn't disrupt other systems?

From a cybersecurity standpoint, we were guided by the fundamentals:

Confidentiality – Could we control and audit data access?

Integrity – How would we ensure the data remained accurate and untampered?

Availability – Would these apps be reliable and resilient under real-world demands?

These early discussions with Leandro didn't just raise flags, they helped us chart the course. They anchored our enthusiasm in technical reality and pushed us to design a model that was not only empowering but sustainable.

So we began designing the framework with both creativity and caution, ambition and accountability.

We didn't have a playbook. But we had a purpose.

And we were ready to build something new.

Step 1: Define the Purpose

The first step was to get crystal clear on what we were trying to accomplish and what we weren't.

This wasn't about turning every employee into a software developer or removing IT from the equation. It wasn't about speed at the expense of security. And it wasn't about reinventing governance.

Our goal was simple: to expand the organization's ability to solve real problems by enabling business users to build their solutions within a structure supported by IT.

We defined the purpose of the Citizen Developer program as:

To enable business users to build digital solutions that solve real problems, with support and oversight from IT, within a structured, secure, and scalable framework.

That sentence became our North Star.

Step 2: Choose the Right Platform

Technology isn't the answer to every challenge, but it matters.

We needed a platform that was low code, cloud native, manageable by IT, and well-integrated with our existing systems. Most importantly, it needed to be user-friendly enough for business users to engage with confidently.

We selected Microsoft Power Platform as our foundation. It offered a complete suite of Power Apps, Power Automate, Power BI, and integrated seamlessly with Microsoft 365 and SAP. Many users were already familiar with parts of the platform, which gave us a head start on adoption.

We later expanded to include Python® for more technically advanced builders and began exploring AI-enhanced tools like Copilot Studio. But we started intentionally with a single, focused platform to keep the pilot manageable and the learning curve reasonable.

Step 3: Introduce a Tiered Model

Not all apps are equal. Some are simple tools used by one person. Others touch core processes, sensitive data, or enterprise systems.

To manage risk and scale intelligently, we created a three-tiered development model:

Tier 1 – Personal and Team Tools

Lightweight apps or automations created by individuals or small teams. They typically involved no sensitive data and had minimal risk. No formal approval was required, though we encouraged users to register their work for visibility.

Tier 2 – Departmental Solutions

Apps that served entire business units and sometimes touched critical systems or data. They required a solution template, a brief review by IT, and documentation. This ensured alignment and provided a layer of support without creating bottlenecks.

Tier 3 – Enterprise or Strategic Applications

Complex, cross-functional, or mission-critical solutions. They required IT sponsorship or co-development and followed a full lifecycle, including security, performance testing, and change management.

This model created clarity for business users and for IT. Everyone knew what level of oversight was required based on the nature of the solution. We didn't slow down innovation, we created boundaries for it to thrive.

Step 4: Define Roles and Responsibilities

A successful framework depends on the people who support it. We outlined three essential roles in our model:

Citizen Developers

Business users who identify problems and take the initiative to solve them using low-code tools. They build apps, automate workflows, and participate in training. They are closest to the work and therefore best positioned to innovate.

IT Champions

Technical advisors are embedded in or aligned with business units. They don't build the solutions themselves, but they provide architectural guidance, unblock access, answer technical questions, and ensure good practices are followed.

Governance Leads

Individuals are responsible for oversight. They ensure compliance with licensing, data usage, and documentation standards. They maintain visibility across the platform and support regular audits or evaluations.

This structure made it possible to scale support. Instead of IT owning every app, they coached and guided citizen developers, shifting from building everything to enabling many.

Step 5: Enable and Support the Builders

Technology and governance alone aren't enough. People need support, resources, and encouragement to build with confidence.

We developed an enablement path with five key components:

Training: Live and self-paced learning opportunities tailored to each platform and user level

Templates: Ready-made app structures, naming conventions, and examples that users could adapt for their needs

Community: A digital space for citizen developers to ask questions, share progress, and learn from one another

Documentation Kits: Lightweight tools to help builders document their solutions and communicate functionality

Office Hours: Weekly time slots where users could get help from IT Champions on challenges they faced

This wasn't just a technical initiative, it was a human one. And people responded. As word spread and success stories emerged, more users stepped forward to learn, build, and contribute.

Step 6: Monitor and Evolve

We knew we had to track impact, not just to satisfy IT, but to improve the program.

We focused on metrics that balanced usage with outcome:

- Number of apps by tier and business area
- Platform adoption rates
- Time saved or processes improved
- Apps using sensitive data (for compliance)
- Retired or deprecated solutions (to track lifecycle)

We didn't try to control every build. Instead, we created visibility. That allowed us to provide support where needed, identify risks early, and showcase the program's growing value to leadership.

A New Kind of Success

Within the first few months, we saw real results.

Matt's team digitized incident reporting, cutting manual effort and enabling cross-country learning through multilingual support. Another team automated 3PL inventory updates, replacing hours of tedious data entry. A third team replaced paper-based maintenance logs with checklists that triggered SAP work orders in real time.

Each win wasn't just a better process. It was a step toward a new way of working.

Business users were no longer waiting in line. They were building. Solving. Owning.

And IT? We weren't chasing them anymore. We were guiding them.

That's what success looked like.

CHAPTER 7

Empowering the Business

When we launched the Citizen Developer framework, we weren't just unsure how people would respond, we were genuinely concerned about how it would land across different parts of the organization, especially in a multi-country context.

We believed in the framework. We knew the potential was there. But we also knew that culture plays a huge role in innovation, and culture doesn't look the same everywhere.

In the U.S., we were confident. We had leaders like Matt who were already supportive of their teams dedicating time to learning new tools and experimenting beyond their job descriptions. There was a cultural acceptance, even encouragement, of working outside one's immediate responsibilities in the service of improvement.

But in South America, we weren't so sure.

We worried that managers might be less receptive to employees spending time on what could be seen as "noncore" activities, that people might be hesitant to experiment without explicit approval, and that the fear of making mistakes or simply being seen as stepping outside their lane would hold them back.

Still, we moved forward with cautious optimism.

And to our surprise, the framework took root faster than we expected.

Not everywhere at once. Not with the same intensity. But it caught on.

Because once people understood that they had permission to build and that IT was backing them, not judging them, something shifted. Tools gave them access. Governance gave them safety. But what made the difference was belief: in themselves, in the program, and in the idea that they could be more than just users.

They didn't wait for a perfect rollout plan.

They got to work.

As the framework took hold, something remarkable began to happen not just in one region or department, but across the company. We began to see practical, impactful solutions emerge from the business, often built by people who had never touched a development platform before. What follows is a closer look at some of the successful use cases that brought this movement to life.

These examples go beyond ideas; they show how empowered individuals across the business turned challenges into solutions, using the very tools and support structure we set in motion.

HR: Turning a Clipboard into a Connected Ecosystem

Before our program, reporting a safety incident meant finding a physical form in the office, filling it out by hand, and delivering it to the safety coordinator, who would later enter it into SAP. If that person was out, the report sat in a pile. Sometimes it got lost. Sometimes it got delayed. And too often, valuable lessons stayed locked in one location.

An HR partner, fresh out of our first citizen development training cohort, knew there had to be a better way.

He built an Incident Reporting App using Power Apps. It allowed employees to submit incidents or near misses from their phones. They could take photos of the issue, dictate a voice note, or type out a description. The app transcribes voice to text and even translates the entry into Spanish and Portuguese, enabling visibility for our teams in Latin America.

The data flowed directly into SAP via API, creating real-time work notifications in the PM module.

This wasn't just a form replacement. It was a digital transformation of how we tracked, reported, and shared safety insights across the company.

The app improved response time. But more than that, it helped create a culture of openness and shared learning. Safety wasn't just reactive, it became collaborative.

Supply Chain: Automating What Once Took Days

In our Supply Chain team, 3PL coordination was one of the most manual and error-prone processes we had.

Every week, massive volumes of containers arrive at U.S. ports. Our logistics team received spreadsheets and emails from 3PL partners confirming delivery, inventory status, or discrepancies. An analyst would manually review them, copy data, and post goods receipts and issues in SAP.

It took 30 to 40 hours a week, spread across multiple staff members. Mistakes were common. And updates were always lagging.

A supply chain analyst, one of our earliest and most enthusiastic citizen developers, built an automation using Power Automate. It scanned incoming emails from 3PL partners, parsed structured data from attachments, and automatically updated SAP inventory records through an intermediate service layer.

The process that once took two days now takes less than two minutes.

Even better, inventory accuracy improved significantly. Downstream teams production planners, customer service, and finance suddenly had a reliable source of truth they could trust.

What began as a time-saving tool became a model for how automation could support core operations.

Operations: Digital Maintenance with Real-Time Triggers

On the shop floor, inspections were still conducted with pen and paper. Operators would walk through the line, mark checkboxes, jot down notes, and submit physical logs at the end of each shift. If they spotted an issue, they'd alert the maintenance team or not. Some things were easy to overlook.

Work orders were often delayed or incomplete. Equipment issues sometimes escalated simply because the process relied on memory and follow-up.

An operations supervisor took it upon himself to change that.

Using Power Apps, he created a set of digital inspection checklists that could be used on a shared tablet. Operators logged their observations in real time. If they flagged a problem, the app would immediately trigger a SAP PM work notification, complete with photos, timestamps, and equipment IDs.

This reduced downtime. But more importantly, it gave the maintenance team better information, allowing them to plan smarter, act faster, and avoid guesswork.

The checklists were so effective that other plants asked to replicate the solution. And that's when something clicked for us:

We weren't just solving isolated problems anymore.

We were creating internal accelerator solutions that could be reused, adapted, and scaled across the business.

Cross-Functional: Proactive Data Quality Monitoring

One of our citizen developers saw a problem nobody fully owned, but everybody felt. Data quality across our ERP systems had always been a challenge. Small inaccuracies, missing fields, incorrect formatting, and duplicate entries often seemed minor at first, but regularly spiraled into significant issues downstream. They caused shipment delays, impacted reporting accuracy, and, worst of all, sometimes affected customers directly.

This citizen developer, who worked at the intersection of Supply Chain and Operations, believed there had to be a proactive way to tackle this issue. She proposed developing automated agents, small, intelligent tools powered by low-code platforms that could continuously monitor key data points across multiple systems. These agents could detect anomalies in real time, flagging potential errors before they propagated further into our processes.

The solution didn't stop at just flagging issues, it took action. Simple errors could be autonomously corrected by the agent itself, based on predefined rules and thresholds. For more complex cases, the agent would instantly alert the responsible data steward or business owner, complete with details about the nature of the problem and recommendations for fixing it.

Within weeks of implementation, the impact was clear. Teams that previously spent hours resolving data-induced headaches saw immediate relief. Inventory accuracy improved. Shipment errors decreased. Customer interactions became smoother and more predictable.

But even beyond these measurable benefits, something deeper emerged: a new sense of shared responsibility for data quality across the organization. Rather than waiting for problems to bubble up and spread, we had found a way to proactively keep our data healthy and trustworthy collaboratively and cross-functionally.

This wasn't just a citizen-developed tool.

It was a citizen-driven shift toward proactive excellence.

Not Just Tools: A Mindset Shift

As more use cases emerged, we noticed something even more powerful than the apps themselves: a change in mindset.

People no longer saw technology as something that belonged to "IT." They saw it as part of how they did their jobs. They weren't afraid of automation. They were hungry for it.

They weren't just thinking, "What can I ask IT to build for me?"

They were thinking, "What can I build to make this easier?"

And IT? We weren't overwhelmed, we were energized. Instead of triaging endless requests, we were coaching, enabling, and guiding.

The Ripple Effect

We started hosting demo days, internal events where citizen developers could showcase what they had built. Participation exploded. Teams clapped for each other. Leaders took notes. We even launched a "Citizen Developer of the Month" recognition program.

Departments began forming mini innovation squads of employees who became known as "the person who could automate that." These weren't formal roles. They were reputations earned through action.

In some cases, career paths shifted. One analyst transitioned into a hybrid business tech role, supporting teams across two regions. Another user became an internal trainer, helping others navigate Power Platform.

What had started as a pilot became a movement.

A culture shift was underway.

It Was Never About the Tools

Looking back, the most surprising part wasn't the quality of the apps, it was the quality of the ownership.

People didn't just build because we gave them the tools. They built because we permitted them. And when we celebrated them, supported them, and showcased their work, they rose to the occasion.

That's what empowerment looks like: not telling people what to do, but giving them the space and support to solve what they already understand best.

CHAPTER 8:

Lessons Learned

By the time our Citizen Developer Program reached maturity, we had dozens of successful solutions, a growing community of builders, and strong executive support.

But make no mistake, it wasn't a straight line.

Behind every win were lessons hard learned. Mistakes made. Assumptions broken. And, most importantly, course corrections that kept the program from derailing.

This chapter is about those lessons, not the theoretical ones, but the ones that came from real conversations, real frustrations, and real growth.

If you're considering your program, I hope these reflections will help you build with more confidence and fewer surprises.

Lesson 1: Access Without Enablement Leads to Chaos

At one point, we made the mistake of opening access to our platform before we were fully ready to support it. Our goal was to move fast. But what we got was confusion.

Some users started building immediately but didn't know about templates, security practices, or support channels. Others didn't know where to begin and gave up entirely. A few solutions made it into production without review and had to be rolled back.

What we learned: Access is just the starting point. Without onboarding, guidance, and clear next steps, most users either stall out or move in the wrong direction.

What we did: We created a structured enablement journey combining training, templates, and office hours so new users didn't feel like they were dropped into a maze.

Lesson 2: Governance Is Not the Enemy

In the beginning, some business users saw governance as bureaucracy. And some IT folks feared that citizen development meant losing control.

Both views were understandable but incomplete.

Good governance didn't slow us down. It made us faster. Because once we had a framework, tiers, templates, naming standards, documentation, it gave people confidence. They knew what was expected. They knew where to start. And they knew they weren't alone.

What we learned: Governance isn't about rules. It's about creating a structure that supports momentum and reduces rework later.

What we did: We embedded governance into every stage of the builder journey, not as a barrier, but as a supportive guide.

Lesson 3: Some Want to Build. Others Want to Contribute. Both Matter.

Not everyone wants to be a citizen developer, and that's okay.

Some employees wanted to learn the platform and build end-to-end. Others wanted to share pain points and ideas, but had no interest in creating the solution themselves. And many just wanted to use what was built.

We realized that all three roles were essential: the builders, the idea generators, and the end users.

What we learned: If you only focus on growing the number of developers, you'll miss the bigger picture and alienate the very people who help make the ecosystem thrive.

What we did: We shifted our success metrics away from "how many people are building" and toward outcomes: time saved, errors reduced, and business value delivered.

Lesson 4: A Few Builders Will Drive Most of the Impact

The 80/20 rule applied here, too. A relatively small group of power builders created the majority of high-impact solutions.

They weren't always the most technical people. But they were curious, committed, and connected to real problems.

Rather than trying to push everyone into training, we started identifying and supporting our high-potential builders early. They became internal champions and helped scale the program organically.

What we learned: Focus on depth before breadth. Empower your early adopters. They'll bring others along faster than any top down mandate.

Early in the program, it was tempting to aim for big numbers: train hundreds of users, launch dozens of apps, cover every business unit. But what we quickly realized is that quantity doesn't create momentum quality does. Our most meaningful progress came not from widespread exposure, but from a few motivated early adopters who saw the value and ran with it.

These individuals didn't just build apps they inspired others. They solved real problems that others could relate to. And because they were peers not external consultants or IT professionals their work was credible. Tangible. Contagious.

Trying to push everyone into the program too soon would have diluted the experience and overwhelmed the support model. Instead, we focused on nurturing a small group of committed champions. They became our proving ground testing the framework, shaping best practices, and generating early success stories that spoke louder than any policy memo.

Their passion was our best marketing.

What we did: We created a spotlight series to recognize top contributors and encouraged them to mentor others across their departments.

To keep that momentum alive and to show that this new way of working was not just allowed, but celebrated we launched a monthly Citizen Developer Spotlight.

Each spotlight featured a different business user who had built something impactful. We shared their story through internal newsletters, town halls, and community calls: what problem they solved, how they approached it, what tools they used, and what impact they achieved.

But we didn't stop at recognition. We invited them to mentor others, lead demos, or co host learning sessions in their departments. Some became informal "innovation leads." Others helped shape our training materials based on their experience.

This created a ripple effect. Builders saw what was possible, users saw who to turn to, and leaders saw proof that grassroots innovation could be scalable, secure, and aligned.

In the end, those early champions didn't just build apps.

They built belief.

Lesson 5: IT Resistance Isn't Personal It's Practical

In some cases, we faced pushback from IT colleagues. Concerns about platform sprawl, duplication, and security risks were real and sometimes frustrating.

But over time, I realized this wasn't resistance for the sake of it. It was protection. IT was tasked with keeping the business running. They'd seen things go wrong. Their skepticism wasn't sabotage. It was caution born of responsibility.

What we learned: IT resistance is often rooted in valid concerns, and those concerns are best addressed through visibility, not secrecy.

At first, we interpreted IT's hesitation as resistance to change. We assumed they were trying to protect their turf or slow down innovation. But over time, we realized something more nuanced: IT wasn't resisting innovation, they were reacting to risk.

From their perspective, the rise of business-led development raised serious and legitimate questions:

- Who's accessing what data?
- What integrations are being created without oversight?
- Are these apps introducing compliance or security gaps?
- Who supports them when something breaks?

And the truth is, they weren't wrong to ask.

While business users were often laser focused on solving immediate problems, IT had to think about what happens next week, next month, next year. Their job wasn't just to support innovation it was to protect the integrity of the entire ecosystem.

When IT is left out of the process or worse, kept in the dark it naturally leads to pushback. But when they have visibility, context, and a clear role to play, their posture changes. What looked like resistance often becomes collaboration.

We didn't need to convince IT to accept citizen development.

We needed to invite them into it.

What we did: We brought IT into the design of the program early. We created dashboards to show platform usage, data sensitivity, and risk levels. And we made them partners, not gatekeepers.

Rather than presenting IT with a finished model and asking for sign off, we brought them into the process early as co-designers.

We asked:

- What would make you feel confident that this is safe?
- What do you need to monitor to sleep at night?
- What kind of oversight would feel like support, not surveillance?

From those conversations, we co-created a governance layer that worked for everyone.

We built dashboards that showed:

- The number and location of active apps
- Data sources being used, especially those touching sensitive information
- Risk tiers, based on access, complexity, and system impact
- Usage trends and potential redundancies

This transparency reduced anxiety. It replaced assumptions with facts. And it gave IT the context they needed to make informed decisions without slowing the pace of development.

Most importantly, we shifted the role of IT from gatekeeper to strategic enabler. They weren't the team that said "no." They were the team that said, "Yes, here's how we'll do it safely."

That simple reframing changed everything.

Lesson 6: If You Don't Create a Feedback Loop, You'll Lose the Trust

One of the first successful apps we launched hit a snag two months later. A form stopped working due to a connector issue. Users submitted feedback through the app, but no one responded.

The builder had moved on. IT wasn't monitoring the app. And the users? They stopped using it.

We nearly lost all the credibility we'd built because no one had ownership after go-live.

What we learned: If there's no clear way for users to report issues and no process for resolving them, you won't just lose the solution. You'll lose trust in the system.

It's easy to celebrate the launch of a new app or automation. But the real test of a solution isn't day one, it's day ninety. That's when the builder has moved on, the initial excitement has faded, and the app becomes part of someone's daily workflow.

And that's when something breaks.

Maybe a data source changes. A platform update disables a connector. A form field behaves unexpectedly. In any traditional IT-managed system, there would be a support model in place. But in a citizen-led ecosystem, support is often ambiguous.

In one case, a business critical app stopped functioning after a platform update. Users tried to report it, but there was no clear point of contact. The original builder had changed roles. IT wasn't tracking the app because it wasn't in their inventory. No one responded, and the app went dormant.

That breakdown wasn't just about functionality, it was about credibility.

People started to question the reliability of the platform.

Worse, they questioned whether anyone was actually in charge.

Trust is the true currency of citizen development.

If users don't believe someone will respond when things go wrong, they stop using what's built and stop believing in the model altogether.

What we did: We added lightweight support expectations, including naming an app owner and setting up automated feedback notifications. We also created a simple "retirement checklist" for decommissioning unused tools.

To prevent silent failures, we put simple but effective safeguards in place.

First, we required that every published app, regardless of tier, have a named owner. This didn't have to be someone from IT, but it did have to be someone accessible, known, and responsible for monitoring the app's performance and feedback.

Second, we introduced automated feedback collection. Within each app, users could click a button to report an issue or suggest an improvement. That feedback was routed directly to the owner, with escalation logic if it went unanswered.

Third, we recognized that not every app should live forever. We created a retirement checklist, a short guide for decommissioning apps that were no longer needed or had been replaced. It included steps for notifying users, archiving data, and updating platform records.

These simple additions made a major difference. Users felt heard. Builders felt supported. I felt informed.

And perhaps most importantly, the program felt sustainable, not just exciting in the beginning, but dependable for the long term.

Lesson 7: Culture Is the Real Platform

The biggest insight of all?

The technology mattered. The governance mattered. But in the end, culture made or broke the program.

From the start, we invested in tools, training, and frameworks. We rolled out structured onboarding, provided clear guidelines, and made sure our citizen developers had what they needed to get started.

And on paper, it worked.

Apps were being built. Automations were improving processes. The feedback was overwhelmingly positive.

But underneath that progress, we began to see a deeper challenge, one that tools alone couldn't fix: culture.

In some parts of the organization, innovation took off. People shared ideas freely, experimented with the platform, and proudly demoed what they built. In others, nothing happened. Even with the same access, the same training, and the same support, things just... stalled.

The difference wasn't technical skill.

It was the environment.

In high-performing teams, there was psychological safety. Managers encouraged experimentation. Failure was seen as part of the process. People weren't afraid to raise their hands.

But in other areas, there was silent hesitation.

Fear of breaking something.

Fear of being seen as overstepping.

Fear of not being "technical enough."

One employee quietly admitted, "I built something, but I didn't want anyone to know in case it wasn't good enough."

That's when it hit us: we couldn't fix cultural hesitation with more code or tighter governance. The barriers weren't technical, they were emotional and organizational.

You can't build your way out of a cultural gap. You have to lead through it.

What We Did

Instead of adding more tools, we focused on shifting leadership behavior.

We sat down with department heads and asked them to do three things:

1. Model the mindset

Speak openly about trying new things, even if imperfect. Normalize experimentation at the leadership level.

2. Celebrate early builders

Publicly recognize team members who took initiative, regardless of outcome. Treat effort as progress.

3. Make innovation part of the job

Stop treating experimentation as an extracurricular. Embed it in performance conversations, in standups, in how work gets done.

We also encouraged leaders to share their own stories, whether they'd tried Power BI, tested an automation, or even failed at something new. That vulnerability made innovation feel human. It told their teams: You don't need to be perfect to get started.

And in the teams where this shift happened, the results were dramatic.

Engagement soared.

Building became a team activity, not a side hustle.

The framework became something people wanted to be part of, not something handed down from IT.

The Real Transformation

We didn't just accelerate adoption.

We helped spark a cultural transformation.

Innovation stopped being something people hid.

It became something they were proud of.

And that, more than any tool or training, is what sustained the movement.

Conclusion: Mistakes Were Inevitable. Giving Up Wasn't.

If there's one message I hope you take from this chapter, it's this:

You will make mistakes. Everyone does.

Some apps won't land.

Some automations will break.

Some people will lose steam halfway through a project.

And that's okay.

Because those aren't failures.

They're signals of growth.

The only real failure is abandoning the opportunity, retreating into old habits because things didn't work perfectly the first time.

Citizen development isn't a plug-and-play solution.

CHAPTER 9

The Future of Work Is Here

We used to think of IT as the engine room of innovation, where technology was built, maintained, and tightly controlled. And for a long time, that model worked.

But the world has changed.

Today, the speed of business outpaces the speed of traditional IT. Customers expect instant responses. Markets shift overnight. Internal processes need to adapt weekly, not yearly.

In this new reality, organizations can't afford to wait.

And that's where citizen development becomes more than a program, it becomes a new operating model.

A New Kind of Workforce

- The workforce is evolving.
- Business users are more comfortable with technology than ever before.
- Cloud tools are accessible and intuitive.
- AI copilots, low-code platforms, and automation engines are becoming everyday tools, not just IT experiments.

This isn't just a digital transformation, it's a talent transformation.

Your future leaders will be the ones who can blend domain expertise with technical curiosity. They won't wait for change, they'll build it.

And your job, as an IT or business leader, is to make that possible safely, strategically, and at scale.

The Role of IT Has Changed Forever

IT will always play a critical role in governance, security, architecture, and enterprise systems. But the expectation has shifted.

You're no longer just the builders.

You're the enablers.

In this new model, IT's value comes not from controlling everything, but from empowering everyone.

By curating tools, enabling frameworks, and guiding governance, IT can become the backbone of a distributed innovation ecosystem, one where business users build, and IT ensures those builds are secure, integrated, and sustainable.

That's not losing control. That's scaling it.

The Power of Co-Creation

Citizen development doesn't mean "business only" development. It means collaboration.

- The best solutions will still come from the intersection of:
- Business users who understand the problem deeply,
- IT professionals who understand the technology deeply,
- And a culture that encourages them to build together.

That's the sweet spot.

That's where transformation happens, not from a software rollout, but from a mindset shift.

What Comes Next?

The future of citizen development isn't just about building apps, it's about building organizational agility and technical fluency at every level of the enterprise.

As the digital landscape evolves, so too does the role of the citizen developer. What began as business-led app creation is expanding into automation, AI, and even operational technology on the shop floor. Citizen development is quickly becoming a foundational strategy for how companies innovate, adapt, and compete.

Here's what we see on the horizon:

AI-Powered Development

The rise of agentic AI platforms like Microsoft Copilot Studio and Google's Gemini is redefining what it means to build. Business users can now create apps, workflows, and dashboards simply by describing what they want in natural language.

AI doesn't just accelerate development, it also lowers the barrier to entry. Even those with no technical background can start solving problems, supported by AI copilots that offer suggestions, validations, and integrations in real time.

Federated Governance Models

As citizen development scales, centralized governance alone won't cut it. Organizations will shift toward federated models, where departments manage their innovation initiatives under a shared set of enterprise standards, platforms, and policies.

IT doesn't disappear, it evolves into an enabler and strategic advisor, helping business-led development happen safely, securely, and sustainably.

Digital Fluency as a Core Skill

We're approaching a future where digital problem solving becomes as essential as using spreadsheets or email. Employees across roles, not just in IT, will be expected to know how to automate tasks, interpret data, and use digital tools to improve workflows.

Digital fluency will no longer be optional; it will be a core expectation.

Hyper Automation Ecosystems

Citizen developers will increasingly work within broader automation ecosystems that include RPA, APIs, data analytics, and AI. The focus won't just be on single solutions but on orchestrating entire business processes end-to-end.

Think: a single flow that connects supply chain updates, inventory alerts, automated messaging, and SAP transactions, all built and maintained collaboratively between IT and the business.

Operational Citizen Development: Bridging IT and OT

One of the most exciting shifts is the extension of citizen development into operational environments, especially on the shop floor. Technicians and engineers are beginning to use low-code tools to digitize checklists, automate inspections, and trigger maintenance events directly from mobile devices.

For example:

- Computer vision tools are being configured by non-developers to detect safety violations or quality issues.

- Collaborative robots (COBOTs) now feature low-code interfaces, enabling shop floor workers to program basic tasks without writing complex code.
- Maintenance teams are building apps that integrate with SAP PM to generate work orders in real time, replacing paper processes with voice, images, and automated translations.

This convergence of citizen development and operational technology (OT) is closing the gap between digital innovation and physical execution.

Embedded Innovation Teams

Finally, we'll see more cross-functional innovation squads embedded directly in business units, blending operational expertise with digital capability. These teams won't rely on traditional project cycles; they'll work continuously, building and improving tools that solve real business problems, with IT as their partner, not their gatekeeper.

The Road Ahead

The future of citizen development is not about replacing IT, it's about expanding the circle of who can build.

Organizations that embrace this shift will:

- Solve problems faster,

- Unlock the potential of their people,
- And create a culture of innovation that runs from the front lines to the boardroom.

The technology is ready. The tools are here. The only question is: Are you ready to empower the builders inside your business?

Your Call to Action

If you're reading this as a business leader, start the conversation. Identify your tech-savvy problem solvers. Give them room to grow. Recognize their potential.

If you're in IT: shift your posture. Be the guide, not the gatekeeper. Build the framework that gives others the confidence to build.

And if you're somewhere in between, someone who understands both the problem and the power of a solution, you might be the next citizen developer.

Don't wait for permission. Start learning. Start building. Start solving.

Because the future of work isn't coming. It's already here.

And it belongs to those who are ready to create it.

CHAPTER 10

When Citizen Development Goes Wrong

L et's be honest.

Not everything went smoothly. Some of our biggest lessons came from what didn't work.

Citizen development has the power to transform organizations. But without structure, it can also expose risks, create confusion, and strain relationships. It's not the tools that fail, it's the absence of boundaries, clarity, and communication.

This chapter isn't about fear. It's about foresight.

Here are the missteps we encountered or narrowly avoided on our journey, and what we learned from each one.

Mistake #1: Opening the Floodgates Too Early

At one point, we made platform access broadly available to the business before our governance model was fully in place. We wanted to drive excitement and adoption, but what we got was a wave of apps, most without documentation, version control, or any kind of oversight.

People were building before they were ready. Others copied apps from each other without understanding how they worked. Some were asking IT to fix what they had built themselves.

It was the very thing we had set out to avoid: a new form of shadow IT, this time backed by sanctioned tools.

What we learned: Access without enablement isn't empowerment, it's exposure.

What we did differently: We paused, regrouped, and launched a structured enablement path, where access was tied to training, templates, and light approval depending on the app's tier.

Mistake #2: Misjudging Governance as a Barrier

At first, we thought "keep it light" would drive adoption. We avoided governance processes to stay agile. But that approach backfired.

As more apps went live, questions started piling up:

- Who owns this?
- Is this version secure?
- Why are there two dashboards with different data?

Without clear ownership, documentation, or naming standards, confusion set in fast.

Ironically, the lack of governance slowed us down more than the presence of it ever would have.

What we learned: Proper governance doesn't limit innovation. It sustains it.

What we did differently: We introduced tiered governance, lightweight for personal apps, tighter for business-critical ones, with self-service templates and peer reviews.

Mistake #3: Assuming Everyone Wants to Be a Developer

One early goal was "every team should have a citizen developer." It sounded great. It looked great on slides. But in reality? Not everyone wants to build.

Some users were happy to suggest ideas. Others were happy just to use the finished tools. A few became true builders.

Trying to push people into roles they didn't want only created frustration and, in some cases, resistance.

What we learned: Contribution takes many forms, and they're all valuable.

What we did differently: We built a three-part model: builders, collaborators (idea contributors), and consumers. Success wasn't just measured in apps built, but in value created across the ecosystem.

Mistake #4: Ignoring IT Concerns (Even the Unspoken Ones)

Some IT leaders were cautious from the beginning, and we didn't always listen closely enough. We assumed their concerns were old-school resistance. But many of them saw risks we hadn't anticipated.

One team was worried about app sprawl. Another flagged access to sensitive finance data. A third pointed out we had no process for decommissioning apps.

They weren't saying "don't do it." They were saying, "Do it responsibly."

What we learned: IT isn't the blocker; they're your firewall. Respect their experience.

What we did differently: We brought IT into the design process early. We created shared dashboards, established clear escalation paths, and aligned on shared success metrics.

Mistake #5: No Ownership After Go Live

In one case, a critical operations app broke when Microsoft rolled out a platform update. No one knew who owned it. The original builder had changed departments. The team using it didn't know how to fix it.

What began as a small outage snowballed into a week of workaround emails and Excel sheets, setting the program back by months in terms of trust.

What we learned: Every app, no matter how small, needs a support plan.

What we did differently: We implemented a lightweight support model that included:

- Naming a clear app owner
- Documenting handoffs
- Sunset plans for unused solutions
- A notification system for major platform changes

Mistake #6: Treating the Program Like a Project

Citizen development isn't a project with an end date. It's a shift in how your organization works.

We learned this the hard way when we let the program coast after a successful first year. Training slowed. Community engagement dropped. The backlog of ideas grew, but support didn't scale with it.

Momentum was lost. It took months to rebuild.

What we learned: This isn't a one-time transformation. It's an ongoing operating model.

What we did differently: We secured long-term sponsorship, embedded enablement into onboarding for new hires, and treated the program like a product with regular updates, community events, and roadmaps.

Bonus Pitfall: Too Many Metrics, Not Enough Meaning

At one point, we celebrated hitting 100 live apps. It was a big milestone, but in truth, many of those apps were redundant, unused, or forgotten.

We were counting quantity, not impact.

What we learned: Activity $\neq$ value.

What we did differently: We shifted to outcome-based metrics, such as:

- Time or cost savings per solution
- User satisfaction
- Solution reuse across departments
- Apps maintained and supported for over six months

These told a far better story of whether citizen development was truly working.

Summary: Failure Isn't the Enemy, Stagnation Is

Every mistake in this chapter could have become a reason to stop.

But we didn't stop. We listened. We learned. We adapted.

The truth is, citizen development will always involve risk. You're distributing innovation into parts of the business that weren't trained to think like developers, and that's okay.

The point isn't to eliminate all risk. It's designed for it.

And when things go wrong? That's not the end of the story. It's the start of the next chapter.

Because if your culture can recover, adapt, and grow, that's not a failure.

That's a breakthrough.

CHAPTER 11

Culture First, Then Code

You can have the best tools. You can have the cleanest governance model. You can even have a dozen great apps in production. But if your culture doesn't support innovation, none of it will last.

Citizen development isn't just a technical change. It's a cultural one. It challenges hierarchy. It blurs traditional boundaries. It asks people to step out of "how we've always done it" and into a new mindset.

And that kind of shift doesn't happen through training alone.

It happens through culture, the shared expectations, beliefs, and behaviors that guide how work gets done every day.

If you want to scale citizen development, start by building the culture that can carry it.

1. Psychological Safety Is the Soil

Innovation can't grow in fear.

If employees feel they'll be punished for trying something new, they won't experiment. If they worry that IT will shut them down or leadership won't support them, they'll retreat.

And when the first thing they build doesn't work perfectly, if the reaction is blame or silence, that might be the last thing they try to build.

Psychological safety isn't about tolerating carelessness, it's about encouraging learning. It's about making it okay to raise your hand, ask a question, or try something new without fear of ridicule or repercussion.

That's where innovation begins.

2. Recognize Effort, Not Just Outcome

Most recognition systems focus on finished products, delivered projects, measurable impact, and quantifiable savings.

But in the early stages of citizen development, the most powerful thing someone can do is start: trying something new, building their first flow, submitting their first use case idea, and helping a colleague understand Power Apps.

If you only recognize outcomes, you'll miss the behavior you want to encourage.

Celebrate effort. Share early stories. Shine a light on people who are figuring it out, even if they haven't reached the finish line yet.

Recognition isn't just about motivation. It's about signaling what your organization truly values.

3. Leadership Sets the Tone

Culture cascades from the top.

If leaders only talk about stability, risk mitigation, and traditional metrics, that's what teams will focus on.

But if leaders share stories of scrappy solutions, call out grassroots innovation, and model curiosity themselves, that sends a different message.

We had one VP who learned how to build a basic Power BI dashboard. It wasn't particularly advanced, but the fact that he built it and shared it in a town hall sent shockwaves through his region.

It told people, "If he can do it, maybe I can too."

When leaders show that it's okay to learn, to try, and to ask questions, the culture follows.

4. Create Time and Space for Innovation

The biggest obstacle to innovation is rarely the interest, it's capacity.

We all have day jobs. Most employees don't have time to explore new tools, learn platforms, or prototype ideas if it's always after hours, after deadlines, after everything else.

If you want people to build, you have to make space for it.

Some organizations offer "innovation hours." Others create rotational roles for citizen developers. We started by simply giving permission, letting managers know it was okay for team members to dedicate part of their time to improving processes.

That signal matters.

If innovation is always an extra, it won't happen. Make it a legitimate part of someone's role, even for 10 percent of their time, and you'll see the results.

5. Flatten the Innovation Hierarchy

In traditional models, innovation happens "up there" in a lab, a strategy office, a center of excellence.

But the best ideas often come from the front lines.

A planner who's been reconciling inventory data for five years. A customer service rep who answers the same question twenty times a day. A technician who's patched the same machine three different ways.

They know the pain. They know what would help. What they need is permission to build or to work alongside someone who can.

When we flatten the hierarchy of innovation, when we say "anyone can improve how we work," we unlock a wave of creativity that was always there, waiting.

6. Shared Language Creates Shared Ownership

How we talk about innovation matters.

Early in our journey, we heard terms like "unauthorized tools," "noncompliant builds," or "unsupported solutions." These words created fear. They framed business users as the problem.

Once we shifted the language, calling them "citizen solutions," "business-led innovation," or "co-created workflows," things changed.

People felt safer. I felt included. Everyone understood this wasn't about rebellion, it was about responsibility.

Language shapes how we see ourselves. Use it wisely.

7. Culture Outlasts Programs

Your citizen development initiative might start with a pilot, a few apps, a few success stories, and a champion in IT.

But if the culture doesn't change, the momentum will fade. The platform will lose traction. The skills will atrophy.

Sustainable innovation comes not from tools or mandates, but from the norms people adopt when no one's watching.

Are people encouraged to improve their work?

Do they believe their voice matters?

Are they trusted to take the first step?

That's culture. And it's the most powerful platform you'll ever build.

Conclusion: Culture Is the True Framework

You can copy a framework. You can replicate a training plan. You can even borrow templates and governance models.

But culture? You have to grow that yourself.

And that starts with leaders who model the mindset, systems that reward it, and a community that reinforces it.

So before you roll out your platform or measure your app count, ask yourself:

- Have we made it safe to build?
- Have we shown people what's possible?
- Are we celebrating the behavior we want to see?

Because at the end of the day, the future of work doesn't begin with code.

It begins with culture.

When people think about citizen development, they often jump straight to platforms, policies, and permissions. And while those are important, they're not what makes the difference between a failed pilot and a lasting movement.

The real engine behind successful citizen development isn't technology. It's culture.

You can train employees, provision environments, and publish governance documents, but if your culture doesn't support creativity, experimentation, and trust, you'll get resistance, not results.

Let's talk about what it really takes to build a culture where citizen development thrives.

1. Psychological Safety Is Non-Negotiable

At the heart of every great innovation culture is psychological safety, the belief that it's okay to try something, share an idea, or even make a mistake without being punished or dismissed.

If your citizen developers are afraid to break something, afraid to look foolish, or afraid to get in trouble for stepping out of their lane, they won't build. They'll stay quiet. They'll wait for permission that may never come.

Leaders must create an environment where experimentation is safe, where learning in public is respected, and where imperfect progress is celebrated.

That's how real momentum starts.

2. Recognize More Than Just Results

In traditional corporate environments, recognition often comes at the finish line when something is launched, implemented, or approved.

But citizen development requires a different kind of recognition:

- Celebrate ideas, not just finished products.

- Spotlight effort and initiative, not just outcomes.
- Acknowledge first attempts, even if they fail.

Why? Because the courage to start is what keeps the movement alive.

Consider:

- Hosting monthly or quarterly "Demo Days" or "Builder Spotlights."
- Sharing stories in internal newsletters or town halls.
- Giving badges, certificates, or even small bonuses to top contributors.

You don't need big budgets. You need consistent visibility and appreciation.

3. Leadership Must Go First

If you want employees to embrace change, your leaders have to model it.

That doesn't mean they need to build apps themselves (although some might surprise you!). It means they need to:

- **Talk openly about citizen development in meetings.** Leaders set the tone. When they speak, people listen not just for directives, but for signals about what matters. That's why one of the simplest but most powerful things a leader can do is talk about citizen development regularly and visibly. Not just in innovation forums, but in everyday team meetings, project updates, and operational reviews. Mention tools that were built internally. Ask questions like, "Has anyone tried automating this?" or "Is this something we could solve with a low-code approach?" When leaders speak the language of innovation casually, confidently, and consistently, it normalizes the behavior across the organization. It shows that this isn't just an IT initiative or side project; it's part of how the business moves forward.

- **Encourage their teams to propose and pilot ideas.** In many organizations, good ideas die in silence, not because people lack creativity, but because they don't feel empowered to act. Effective leaders actively invite their teams to identify pain points and propose solutions, even if they're rough, unpolished, or incomplete. And more importantly, they give those ideas space to breathe. This might mean carving out time for experimentation, sponsoring a pilot, or simply giving public encouragement to someone who tried something new. It's not about perfection, it's about momentum. Leaders who encourage pilots signal that innovation is safe, expected, and valued. And those pilots, however small, often lead to breakthroughs that ripple far beyond the original use case.

- **Remove roadblocks when someone takes initiative.** Nothing kills motivation faster than friction. A builder has an idea, starts a prototype, and suddenly hits a wall: access is denied, data isn't available, or approvals are stuck in a black hole. That's where leadership makes all the difference. When someone takes initiative, leaders must act as accelerators, not just spectators. That means clearing access issues, aligning stakeholders, or advocating with IT or compliance teams when necessary. Even something as simple as saying, "Let's figure out how to unblock this," can be transformative. When employees see that their leaders have their backs, they take more risks, push more boundaries, and ultimately, drive more meaningful change.

When a department leader celebrates a homegrown solution instead of defaulting to an IT request, that sends a powerful message.

Culture shifts when leadership signals that this matters not just in strategy decks, but in daily behavior.

4. Cross-Functional Collaboration Needs to Be the Norm

Citizen development naturally blurs the lines between IT and business, between operations and data, between traditional silos.

That's a good thing, but only if your culture supports it.

If your teams are used to working in isolation, protecting turf, or defaulting to "this is not my job," then collaboration becomes a battle.

But when the culture values shared ownership and problem solving, citizen development becomes a bridge, not a battleground.

Encourage mixed working groups. Create shared spaces for ideation. Reward team wins, not just individual ones.

5. Make Innovation Part of the Job Description

In many companies, innovation is treated like a side project, something you do if you have extra time. Which, of course, no one ever does.

To sustain citizen development, you need to make space for it. That might mean:

- Allowing employees to spend 10–20 percent of their time on improvement initiatives
- Including "contribution to digital innovation" in performance reviews
- Defining career paths that reward creative problem solving

When innovation is baked into the role, not added on top of it, it becomes part of how the business runs.

6. Align with Purpose, Not Just Process

People are more motivated when they understand the "why" behind what they're doing.

Citizen development isn't just about faster apps or fewer IT tickets. It's about:

- Giving teams more control over their tools
- Eliminating frustrating manual work
- Creating better experiences for colleagues and customers

Make sure your program connects to real problems and real impact. Don't lead with platforms, lead with purpose.

When people see that what they build makes a difference, they invest more.

7. Language Shapes Behavior

Culture is reinforced by what people say and how they say it.

If your internal communication still uses terms like:

- "Unapproved development"
- "Unauthorized tools"
- "End user development risk"

…you're unintentionally framing citizen developers as a problem.

Shift your language to reflect trust and empowerment:

- "Business-led innovation"
- "Citizen solutions"
- "Co-created workflows"

Language matters. It either opens doors or closes them.

Conclusion: Culture Is the Platform

In citizen development, platforms matter. Governance matters. Training matters.

But culture is what makes it all stick.

Without the right culture, you'll get isolated wins that fade away.

With the right culture, you'll get a movement that scales, evolves, and becomes a natural part of how your organization thinks, works, and grows.

So before you code anything, ask yourself:

- Do we reward curiosity?
- Do we tolerate mistakes?
- Do we celebrate learning?
- Do we trust our people to solve problems?

Because the success of your program doesn't begin with an app. It begins with a mindset.

And that mindset is something you build together.

CHAPTER 12

Managing the Change Before the Change Manages You

You can have the right tools.

You can have the right framework.

But if you don't manage the human side of change, none of it will stick.

When we launched the Citizen Developer framework, we weren't just introducing a new way of building solutions. We were challenging deeply held beliefs about ownership, responsibility, and risk. We were asking people to rethink their role, not just in IT, but in innovation itself.

And that kind of shift doesn't happen automatically.

The Truth About Change

Most resistance isn't about the idea itself.

It's about what the idea represents:

- Loss of control
- Fear of the unknown
- Extra workload
- Being made obsolete

We saw it immediately. Some managers feared they'd lose authority. Some IT teams worried they'd be buried in bad code. Some employees just didn't want "one more thing" on their plate.

None of this was irrational. It was human.

That's why we knew early on: this had to be a change initiative, not just a technology initiative.

Creating a Movement, Not Just a Mandate

We didn't issue a top-down decree. We told a story.

We highlighted pain points that the business already knew, such as weeks-long waits for basic automations, duplicated efforts, and disconnected spreadsheets. We asked a simple question: What if you could fix this yourself?

Then we backed it up with real, relatable examples.

We showed early wins, not big visions.

We didn't promise transformation. We promised traction.

That's how movements begin, not by pushing change, but by pulling people into a better way of working.

Building Trust Through Inclusion

One of the biggest lessons in change management is this: People support what they help create.

So we brought stakeholders into the process from the beginning. Business users helped shape the framework. IT helped define the boundaries. Risk and Security gave input on the safeguards.

When we presented the final model, no one felt ambushed.

They saw their fingerprints on it.

And that made all the difference.

Supporting Adoption, Step by Step

Change isn't a one-time event. It's a process.

So we built a multi-layered enablement plan:

- **Training:** Not just on the tools, but on how to identify automatable problems
- **Mentorship:** IT Champions who could guide business users through their first builds
- **Showcases:** Monthly demos where teams shared what they had built and how it helped
- **Recognition:** Leaders calling out innovation in performance reviews and team meetings

Each of these actions reinforced the message: This is safe. This is supported. And this matters.

Facing Resistance Head On

Even with the right scaffolding, not everyone came along immediately.

Some leaders saw the program as a threat, afraid it would highlight gaps in their teams or erode their control. Others simply didn't see the value.

We didn't try to argue them into alignment.

We let results speak for themselves.

One skeptical department head changed his tune the day his team built a Power App that cut their invoice processing time in half. Another started asking questions after seeing a dashboard his junior analyst created, one that IT hadn't had time to deliver in over a year.

Change often spreads sideways before it moves upward.

We learned to be patient. To keep showing value. To stay consistent.

What Worked and What We'd Do Differently

What worked: Leading with empathy, not urgency

Bringing skeptics into the process instead of leaving them behind

Celebrating early adopters loudly and often

What we'd do differently: Start aligning leadership expectations sooner

Build a formal communication plan from day one

Identify "blockers" and "boosters" across departments early and tailor strategies accordingly

The Takeaway

Citizen development isn't just a technical evolution. It's a cultural one.

And like all cultural change, it requires clarity, patience, empathy, and a plan.

We didn't manage to change perfectly. No one ever does.

But by treating it as core to the success of the program, not an afterthought, we gave ourselves a real chance.

A chance to shift not just how people build, but how they think.

Change doesn't happen because you have a better idea; it happens. After all, you help people believe that the new way is worth the effort to change.

CHAPTER 13

From Builders to Orchestrators: The AI Revolution in Citizen Development

When we began this journey, citizen development was about giving business users the power to build their solutions using low-code and no-code tools. That alone was revolutionary. It changed how organizations operated and who got to participate in digital transformation.

But something even bigger is now unfolding.

As we move through 2025 and beyond, we're witnessing a shift even more profound than low-code platforms: the rise of generative AI and agentic systems technologies that can not only build with us but increasingly think and act alongside us.

We're entering a world where the builder may no longer need to "build" in the traditional sense. Instead, they'll describe, prompt, and orchestrate guiding AI agents that do the heavy lifting of generation, iteration, and optimization.

It's no longer just about citizen developers.

It's about AI augmented problem solvers.

From Drag and Drop to Prompt and Refine

A few years ago, learning a platform like Power Apps was a big leap for most business users. It involved understanding data structures, UI logic, integrations, and more. Templates helped, but building still required hands-on time and a learning curve.

Now, with generative AI tools like Microsoft Copilot Studio, Google Gemini, and ChatGPT, that experience is changing dramatically.

Today, a user can type (or say):

"Create a leave request app that integrates with our HR system, sends an approval to the manager, logs the request in a SharePoint list, and notifies the employee when it's approved."

And the AI responds with a working prototype built in seconds, complete with UI, workflows, and data connections.

Tomorrow, they won't just prompt once. They'll engage in a conversation:

"Make the form mobile-friendly." "Add a weekend restriction to the date picker." "Translate responses into Spanish and Portuguese." "Connect to SAP and trigger a work order when the incident severity is high."

This is the future: not replacing human creativity, but amplifying it.

We are moving from *building with tools* to *collaborating with intelligence.*

Enter the Age of Agentic AI

And the next leap? It's already taking shape.

Agentic AI refers to systems that don't just generate content in response to a single prompt, they carry out goals across multiple steps, tools, and systems with minimal human involvement.

Imagine this:

- You give the AI a goal:

"Create a weekly sales summary dashboard that pulls data from Salesforce, Google Sheets, and SAP."

- The AI plans the steps, gathers the data, builds the pipeline, and asks clarifying questions along the way.
- It schedules updates, sets up permissions, and even alerts you if the data quality is off.

In this world, you're not coding or dragging blocks. You're setting intent and managing the agents that carry it out.

That's not science fiction. It's already in motion.

The Rise of Prompt Engineering

In this new model, prompting becomes a business skill.

Much like we learned to write formulas in Excel, business users will need to learn how to write *effective instructions* for AI. This means understanding:

- How to break down a problem into clear, structured tasks
- How to give the AI context so that it can work with
- How to refine and iterate through conversational feedback

- How to validate results and ensure alignment with goals

We won't need everyone to become programmers. But we will need them to become **strategic communicators of intent**.

Prompt engineering isn't just a tech skill, it's a leadership skill. It's about defining the outcome, guiding the system, and knowing what "good" looks like.

What Doesn't Change

Despite all this evolution, some truths remain:

- **Governance still matters.** The faster we move, the more guardrails we need. AI can generate risky logic just as easily as it can generate useful automation. We'll need human oversight more than ever.
- **Trust is still earned.** AI will get better, but trust comes from results. Teams must still validate, monitor, and take ownership of what has been built.
- **Culture still leads.** Even with AI, experimentation requires safety. Creativity requires space. And adoption requires belief.

The core of citizen development, empowerment, curiosity, and business ownership doesn't go away.

It evolves.

What to Do Now

If you're leading or scaling a citizen development initiative, here's how to prepare for what's next:

1. **Train for prompting**

   Teach people how to describe problems clearly, break down logic, and engage with AI tools through iterative feedback.

2. **Expand the definition of a builder**

3. Accept that not everyone will be hands-on with platforms. Some will prompt, some will test, some will orchestrate. All are valuable.

4. **Create AI governance alongside app governance**

   Develop policies around how AI is used in building, what data it accesses, and how outputs are reviewed and approved.

5. **Experiment early**

   Don't wait for the technology to be perfect. Start small, learn fast, and involve cross-functional teams in shaping how AI is used in your workflows.

6. **Center human judgment**

   Use AI to accelerate solutions but ensure **humans stay in the loop** for ethical, strategic, and contextual decisions.

Final Thought: Human + AI Is the New Platform

Low-code platforms opened the door to a broader generation of builders.

AI is blowing that door off its hinges.

But the future isn't just about automation. It's about **augmentation** humans and machines working in tandem to solve problems, build systems, and improve work faster than ever before.

Citizen development showed us that problem-solving doesn't belong only to IT.

Now, AI is showing us that building doesn't belong only to builders.

The future of innovation is not about who codes. It's about who thinks boldly and acts intentionally.

And that's a future we're all invited to help shape.

CHAPTER 14

The Toolkit & Playbook

By now, you've heard the stories, seen the risks, and hopefully caught the vision of what's possible when business users are empowered to build solutions responsibly.

This chapter is about turning intention into action.

Whether you're preparing to launch your citizen development program or looking to improve an existing one, this toolkit is designed to help you move forward with confidence.

You don't need to adopt every element at once, but you do need to start somewhere and start intentionally.

This playbook outlines the essential elements we used to go from idea to execution.

1. Define Your Purpose

Start with a single, clear sentence that anchors your program.

Here's an example:

"To enable business users to build digital solutions that solve real problems, with support and oversight from IT, within a structured, secure, and scalable framework."

This statement should:

- Clarify the value to the business

- Signal alignment with IT
- Set expectations for how citizen development fits into the larger digital strategy

Your purpose will guide how you prioritize, govern, and communicate.

2. Establish a Tiered Model for Solutions

Not all apps need the same level of review or control. Use tiers to categorize development based on risk and reach.

Tier 1 – Personal or Team Tools

- Low complexity
- No sensitive data
- No approval required, but registration encouraged

Tier 2 – Departmental Solutions

- Medium complexity or impact
- May access operational data
- Requires review and lightweight documentation

Tier 3 – Enterprise or Strategic Solutions

- High complexity or integration
- Touches critical systems or regulated data

- Requires IT sponsorship, lifecycle planning, and formal support

Tiers help scale governance while preserving agility.

3. Define Roles and Responsibilities

Clearly outline the roles that make citizen development sustainable.

Citizen Developer

- Builds apps or automations
- Participates in training
- Follows platform guidelines

IT Champion

- Provides coaching and architectural support
- Reviews Tier 2+ solutions
- Ensures platform alignment

Governance Lead

- Monitors app portfolio and platform activity
- Enforces data and documentation policies
- Coordinates audits and performance reviews

A successful program relies on shared accountability across all three roles.

4. Create an Enablement Path

To turn interest into action, offer structured support:

- **Training Tracks**: Beginner to advanced, including platform fundamentals, security basics, and design thinking
- **Templates**: Pre built app scaffolds, naming conventions, and documentation checklists
- **Community**: Internal forums or groups for peer help, discussion, and recognition
- **Office Hours**: Weekly sessions with IT support for live troubleshooting
- **Resource Hub**: Centralized location for guides, standards, and reusable components

Enablement isn't a one time workshop. It's an ecosystem.

5. Build a Governance Foundation

A light but clear governance structure keeps the program from becoming shadow IT 2.0.

Key elements include:

- Platform usage policy (who can build, where, and with what data)
- Environment strategy (dev/test/prod or business specific sandboxes)
- Approval process tied to app tiers

- Documentation requirements for Tier 2 and Tier 3 apps
- Change management for high impact solutions

Governance shouldn't block building. It should make it safer.

6. Launch a Pilot

Start small, learn fast, and build credibility early.

Pilot program checklist:

- Identify 2–3 departments with strong business leaders and obvious pain points
- Select 3–5 impactful use cases to prototype
- Assign IT champions to support each builder
- Collect metrics on time saved, process improvements, and adoption
- Document lessons learned to improve your framework before scaling

A successful pilot builds confidence across the organization.

7. Track the Right Metrics

Avoid vanity metrics. Focus on indicators of real value.

What to measure:

- Hours or cost saved through automation
- Number of business units participating

- User satisfaction or engagement scores
- Solution adoption and reusability
- Time from idea to production
- Ratio of active builders to supported apps

Dashboards don't need to be complex. They just need to drive the right conversations.

8. Reinforce Through Culture

Citizen development works best when supported by leadership and embedded in how the organization operates.

Tactics for long term success:

- Share builder success stories regularly
- Include digital fluency in performance expectations
- Recognize effort publicly, not just outcomes
- Normalize "10% time" for innovation in key roles
- Appoint internal champions in each business unit

When people see innovation modeled, recognized, and rewarded, it spreads.

9. Plan for Growth and Maintenance

Citizen development is not a "set and forget" program. As adoption grows, so will your responsibility to support and evolve it.

Ongoing needs:

- Regular review of active apps (e.g., quarterly)

- Retiring or upgrading solutions that no longer meet business needs
- Updating training materials and templates as the platform evolves
- Scaling the governance committee or platform team as needed

Future proofing means building with sustainability in mind from day one.

Final Words: This Is Your Starting Line

There's no single right way to implement citizen development. What matters is that you approach it with intention, clarity, and a commitment to learning as you go. This toolkit isn't meant to be rigid. It's meant to give you structure without stifling creativity. Guardrails without red tape.

So take what fits. Modify what doesn't. And most of all get started. Because the future of work belongs to builders. And with the right framework, your people are more ready than you think.

EPILOGUE

From Shadow to Shine

When I look back on this journey from the early days of shadow IT to the structured, supported, and AI augmented world we now find ourselves in one truth stands out more clearly than ever:

This was never just about technology.

It was about people.

People who were tired of waiting. People who saw problems and couldn't look away. People who believed they could do more if only someone would give them permission.

I was one of those people.

I didn't start in IT. I didn't have a formal title that said "architect," "developer," or "innovator." But I had a laptop, a question, and a drive to improve things. That drive led me through success and failure, praise and pushback, confidence and crisis.

And it led me here.

To a place where I've seen firsthand what happens when we stop trying to control innovation and start enabling it. When we stop building systems just for efficiency and start building capacity. When we realize that transformation doesn't come from the top or the center.

It comes from the edges.

From the floor of a plant. From a safety officer with a better idea. From an HR partner with a messy onboarding process and the courage to fix it. From people who know the pain points best because they live them every day.

If this book has shown you anything, I hope it's that you don't need to be a developer to build something that matters. You just need curiosity, support, and space to try.

And now with AI, with low code, with everything we've learned we have the tools.

What we need next are the mindsets.

The mindset to think beyond your role.

The mindset to partner across boundaries.

The mindset to ask not just *"Can I build this?"* but *"What impact will it have?"*

Because the real shift isn't from code to no code.

It's from control to trust, from rigidity to resilience, from shadow to shine.

And that shift starts with people like you.

Made in the USA
Columbia, SC
24 June 2025

59831353R00070